RHYMES WITH WHAT

Rhymes with Wordplay, Humour, Anger and Truth as ingredients

RAJU SUNDARARAJAN

While on the matter of Dedication I am at,

I should like to hasten to Affirm that:

In my mind, my son is ever the first;

And if I love him more, my heart would surely burst.

This book is for my son Harish, ever dutiful and kind;

Always First & Foremost In Raju's Mind.

Contents

Contents

Contents

HALLO, I'M NOT WEANED OFF FREDERIC OGDEN NASH

• 1 •

Having read some of Frederic Ogden Nash's works,
And having a liking for word-coinings, originality and quirks;
I, from time to time, wrote some rhymes of my own,
Hoping that they'd produce giggles and not too many a groan.

Reader, gnash not your teeth over crazy spellings and FONetics;
My goal is always to get treats out of wordplay and lingual tricks;
With any, even a disputable or disreputable pun or rhyme;
That's the aim of my verses - all the time.

For I always have Nashty verses in my head, dear kin and kith;
And impishness is ever an ingredient of the ink I write with.

MAKING FRIENDS WITH THE YOUNGER GENERATION

• 2 •

The early bird catches the early worm;

The early angler catches the early-morning germ;

The early fish latches on to the early-morning worm-bait;

So, unless you are a lark, or doing it for a lark, never get up till it's after eight.

THE MICRO-MINDED MACROLOGIST

• 3 •

The bigoted bore builds a bulwark around his mind;
He keeps it insulated, left and right, front and behind;
Nothing, be it of airplane, or even a hairpin;
Nothing, nothing ever penetrates in.

He maintains his mind on a starvation diet;
Yet he hasn't a qualm about being unquiet.
Into his mind, a moth-like input;
And out his mouth, such mammoth output!

Let's hasten to teach him that brevity is the soul of wit;
And that, in particular, it should ever be the goal of a twit.

LET'S GOSSIP IN GREEK

Years and years of eavesdropping;
Having made her hearing so acute;
She even hears leaves dropping;
A happening which, to us, is mute.

Though I speak in a low tone;
As soon as I lay down my phone;
I am swiftly and surely cornered;
And information is sought to be garnered,
With: Who, What, Why, When, How, and Where;
To answer any is to step straight into a snare.

So don't be vext when you phone next;
And I return the call with a text.
I do it for all, and all the time;
And with reason; but with or without rhyme.

And if you insist that we should speak;
Come then, let's go learn Ancient Greek.

HEY DOC, DON'T THINK I INTEND TO MOCK

Though it's a big bore, living with disease;
Still, the thought of going to the docs fills me with unease.
When I see them amidst their gear;
I'm bewildered, sometimes filled with fear.

When the doc gets into his stethoscope;
Methinks this machine I know, I can cope.
But when he takes in hand the rubber hammer;
I lose my nerve, I begin to stammer.

And when he ties on his mask;
I know he's gonna do a nasty task.
Nasty for him, and nasty for me;
Yet he does it, for sake of the fee.

But the sight that I least love;
Is that of a doc with mask and single glove.
For he, without a word apologetical;
Is gonna do things proctological.

WATCH THE WATCH

Being something of a morning lark;
I used to turn up early for wark.
But as to working at hours late;
I resolved: Never, whatever be the staying rate.

But nothing, it seems, is in my hands;
Not even my watch, which once slipped off i ts bands;
Fell, and under my chair came to a rest;
And this, I now tell my friends, in jest;
Was the only time,
I worked
    time.

Soon after my watch fell, there was a power cut;
And, there being no use waiting, I got off my butt;
And clean forgetting the watch, took a bus home;
And soon was deep in sleep in my bed of foam.

Watchless, I clocked in late the next morn;
By then the cleaning woman had come and gorn;
As soon as I opened my cabin door;
I saw my watch on the floor;
Covering its face with its hands because of dust;
But sound of body and limb, and robust.

That evening as I sat in the homeward bus;
I couldn't help thinking thus:
Had the cleaner been watchful in doing her dooty;
She could have cleaned up a nice bit of booty.

PLURAL AND PUN

A man's mind, thus it is apt to run;
Expressed in the form of plural and pun:

If the plural of mouse,
Is mice;
And that of louse,
Is lice;
More than one spouse,
Should surely be spice.

Life is to be enjoyed in bits of here-and-nows;
And for it to be serene and smooth and nice;
Keep not the spice in one house;
But lodge them far apart in different hice.

Life then becomes a series of wows;
It matters not if it's a bit tainted by vice.

TEN ANTS AND HOSE OWNERS

If some, say, half a score ants;
Climb up the inside of your pants;
Don't haw and hem;
Just aim and pee on them.
When you have finished your task;
Someone would be sure to ask:
"Why all this mess and bother, dear brother?";
Just say: "To protect that which makes a maid a mother."

ANTICS WITH ONOMASTICS

It sometimes seems to me;
That ants may be;
Of various castes and classes;
Just like the human masses.

In the following word-game;
Of ant types I should like to tell;
And also their most likely name;
It's up to you to make the list swell.

The first ant was - Adamant;
The first ant's amusemant - Eve ant;
The resultant - many a descendant.

The joy of this game of verbal gymnastics;
Is to ponder their descendants' onomastics:

The priest, he may be called - Chant;
The warrior, Valiant;
The merchant, Exorbitant;
The menial, Servant;
The beggar, Mendicant;
The contemptible, Pissant;
The dictator, Tyrant;
The distiller, Intoxicant;
The farmer, Peasant;

The foreigner, Important;
The male model, Flamboyant;
The purist, Pedant;
The watchman, Vigilant;
The wrongdoer, Miscreant;
The World War One veteran, Trenchant.

And, at the end of World War Three,
When all other souls have been set free,
The last ant would be:
Remnant.

I THINK: "I AM CLAD"; THEREFORE I AM – GLAD

Some, with heart sincere and kind;
When an important day comes to mind;
Ask me to send them my shirt size;
But I don't, though I could in a trice.

For, from the rat race, a long time ago I've resigned;
So I have no use for new garments, signed or designed.
In fact, most my garments I've put into the "For Charity" bin;
And am perfectly content with what at this moment I'm in.

PERHAPS SOME APPS MAY HELP

A man I know wonders if there be any Apps;
Under the classification "Homes-interiors Maps".

Outside the front door, his wife knows her way about;
And roams the vast city sans fear or doubt.
From the most primitive party-hall;
To the most stupendous shopping mall;
She knows the lot, one and all;
The extra large, the medium, and the very small.

Her wanderings to and fro drains her body batteries;
So she recharges at elegant purse-slimming eateries.

Then, laden with packets, she comes home late;
And recounts her conquests to her sullen mate.
The man, to know just one thing, is really itchin';
And that is: Does this woman know the route to our kitchin?

VILE VICIOUS VINDICTIVE VITUPERATIVE VIRAGO

• 14 •

Though it's much hard to find, from Beijing to the Bahamas;
Yet she has one such - a mind just like Osama's;
It's nothing but a bin laden with hatred and rage;
And constantly on the lookout for a war to wage.
And foremost among her victims of terror;
Is her husband - in her eyes, Evolution's terrible error.

THE SAGE AND THE SELLER

The sage says, "It's great to have the things, by money bought;
"But better still is, not to lose those which, buy it cannot."

However, the seller of pricey apparel from far and near;
Wouldn't like the public, this petty quote to hear.

NONSENSICAL! EXTRAVAGANT! WASTEFUL! STUPIDITY!

• 16 •

At home, whenever I open my mouth;

I hear dissonance from N, E, W, and South.

I have therefore downed the shutter;

On the organs that utter.

CONSULTATIONS, ANYONE?

In matters of tax;
Pray, do not be lax;
Consult a Chartered Accountant;
For he views a thing from many a slant.
Pay him his moderate, reasonable fee;
And conclude your meeting with a friendly cup of tea.

In matters of duty, or dharma;
Or for accumulation of good karma;
Consult your Conscience Always;
And speed up good work with God's blessings and grace.

But in all matters it would be much safer;
For the inveterate invertebrate bow-and-scraper;
To consult his wedded Controlling Authority;
Who invariably imparts instructions with such self-centered ingenuity.

TIME IS MONEY TO MANY

East, West, North and South - in all areas geographic;
The time wasted at our splendid banks is truly horrific.

Since I'm not like PGW's Bertie Wooster;
I can think and act on my own;
I'm not in need of a man-servant or thought-booster;
So, in future, I may myself cache my cash the way a dog does a bone.

THE EX-SOLDIER VISITS HIS BANK

This is a tale about a geriatric pensioner;
Formerly a valiant, dashing, ferocious soldier;
He, in the days, good, old, and fine;
Verily had a ramrod in place of a spine.
His was a hand that hoisted the tricolour over reconquered land;
But now his hypo-DoB makes necessary a tripod in an enfeebled hand;
This gent is now spent and bent with age;
His life's in the last chapter, perhaps even the very last page.

Early this morning he awoke in a sweat from his slumber;
And thinking: "Must secure a ticket with a single-digit number";
Spruced himself up, and to his bank was totteringly gone;
Even when the morn was still soft and silent and newborn.

Working hours commence at 9:30, so the bank says;
The public think that, without discussions and delays;
The customer before Ticket Number 2;
Promptly at 9:30, would be attended to.

However, the bank's staff take it to mean;
That the cranking up of the outer shutter is to be seen;
To commence at workday morning 9:30;
Argue the point, and they're apt to get shirty.

While customers arrive in flocks;
Various incompatible keys and locks;
Are mismatched, then matched, and finally granted divorce;
Not gently, but with facial frown and fingerial force.

But before the public can enter the room;
There appears an impartial and indifferent broom;
And yesterday's dust and today's customer;
Are alike swept out before one can demur.

On entering, the staff firmly press on the workday throttles;
Crediting the water cooler and debiting staff water bottles;
Then they share rumours, mostly half-lies;
And exchange news, neither necessary nor nice.

Then follows a long period during which;
Complex machinery suffer many a glitch;
Sullen, silent computers refuse to boot;
Then the tardy techie's told to troubleshoot.

While still the computers refuse to boot;
The customers discuss a point, by no means moot:
Knowledge of banking, is it the more urgent;
Or of hardware, for all staff, both lady and gent.

The computers at last are given a lease of life;
But it's not time yet to celebrate with drum and fife;
Because connections, rodent-ravaged, or wringably wet,
Delay the start, and the staff call out in glee, "No net".

Finally, however, the squawking of the ticket-machine begins;
With an intonation that would horrify Henry Higgins;
The ex-soldier's ticket number is called;
And at once the old gentleman feels appalled.

For, he has let fall the paper ticket from his fingers;
Cos in his aged and tired frame sleep still lingers;
And experience tells him what he is in for;
But he marches to the counter with a weary "Oh Lor'".

Up at the wicket they scold: "Your ticket, why don't you hold?"
He is the target of a volley of vituperation, uncontrolled;
All this, because a heinous crime he has done, you see;
And that was to misplace the bank's precious property.

His position now reduced to: Beg Before Wicket;
He says: "Sorry, on my forehead I should've stuck it."
But he thinks: "Get my work done, ladies and gents;
"Before I'm spoken of in the past tense."

He has come for neither deposit nor withdraw'l;
But this long has tenanted the banking hall;
Only because he wants a pass-book updation;
But what he gets is a browbeating and beration.

In his prime he has been in the front in many an encounter;
But now he retreats, backs off from the counter;
To seek redress, he rushes from pillar to post;
But in his haste he falls down, and nearly gives up the ghost.

The petrified public think: "We wouldn't be amazed;
"To learn that the staff have among themselves raised;
"A fund with which to buy a ferocious dog;
"To chain to the front door in fine weather and fog;
"This, to free themselves by keeping all customers at bay;
"And then, grant themselves loans, day after working day;
"The only reason they haven't done it so far;
"Is the fear that its barking would on their nerves, jar;
"And deny them their beauty sleep;
"Without which, their rosy complexions, they couldn't keep."

After a hard morning of getting up, and getting ready;
And getting to the office, with surliness burning steady;
The staff think they are entitled to some rest and repose;
But what really results is a condition quite comatose.

Soon thereafter, all work comes to a grinding halt;
For the staff are tired, after mounting many an assault;
They go off to grind their lunches;
Not one by one, but in beaming bonhomous bunches.

Such were the happenings in the bank this a.m.;
Even under the direct supervision of the A.B.M.;
And the public wonder if the spying screen was given to the HoB;
Only as a pre-requisite and a perquisite for his taking the job.

Bank's Directors, come incognito like kings of yore;
Station yourselves outside the front door;
Show this piece to your customers, sore;
They'd agree, then wish to add much more.

LINES WRITTEN ON TWOSDAY, 22/2/22

• 24 •

The sum of 2 and 2 is four;

2 crossing swords with 2 produces the same as before;

And when 2 piggybacks on 2, it doesn't make the answer soar;

But place them side by side and the result is much much much mucher more.

In your minds, the following is the lesson that I wish to plant:

Fax your data, then kindly aks the tax consultant;

And he's sure to view your figure from many a slant;

And your tax-saving - he'll grow it from ant to elephant.

HERS AND HERR'S

He errs when he says all of hers and all of his are the same;
It's certainly true as regards the surname;
But when he said "all", he must have been in a rush;
For I think he never thought of the toothbrush.

MEDICAL MAXIM FOR THE NEW MILLENIUM

• 26 •

Were William Osler here today,
He may have this to say:

Whether his diet be one of wheat or rice,
The person who takes medicine must recover thrice:

Once from the disease,
For which the doctor was given the fees;

Once from the medicine,
Which is mostly fit only for the waste bin;

And once from the shock of seeing his bank balance –
Liquid funds depleted, not drop by drop, but by gallons and gallons.

Note the original quote:
Sir William Osler (1849-1919) said:
"The person who takes medicine must recover twice,
once from the disease, and once from the medicine."

LOOK BEFORE YOU PEEL

Did you know that calendars fret and worry,
On account of flighty, inconstant February?
The Mighty Tree of Eternity,
Out of its fruits aplenty;
Gave February days eight and twenty;
But Feb would rather have one-half of swenty;
It envies its neighbours - they have three days more,
Than its allotment of full weeks four.

Therefore, once in a while, to pluck more, it takes a leap;
And this I come to know when one morn I get up from sleep;
And being neither lazy nor a shirk;
Make ready to march off to work;
And am told by a voice that is not mine:
"Today's not One, it's Twenty-nine;
"So don't peel off the lovely calendar page;
"This year Febby has more dates than we had in teenage."

THE GURKHA

Were he here today, Sam ("Bahadur") Manekshaw;
He might thus express a truth, unadorned and raw:
If a man says he is not afraid of losing his life;
He is a liar; or, could be a man with a shrewish wife;
Or he is - that brave, loyal, little bundle of mirth - the Gurkha.

Note the original quote:
Former Indian Army Chief of Staff
Field Marshal S H F J Manekshaw (1914-2008) said:
"If a man says he is not afraid of dying, he is either lying or he is a
Gurkha."

A SALUTE TO THE HAPPY WARRIOR

The Gurkha is a tiny little chap;

His homeland's a tiny oblong in the world map.

He has a face like a wide-smile smiley;

And he is neither obsequious nor wily.

He treats all as equals, the whole of humanity:

Rich man, poor man, cobbler and celebrity.

He stands straight, and looks you in the eye;

Whether you talk long, or just say hi or bye.

To a company's chairman, he does not kowtow;

At a charwoman he does not bark out a "bow wow".

The Gurkha is ever true to his salt;

And stands unflinching under assault.

He is the merriest of the merry in ordinary life;

But in battle wields the fearsome kukri knife.

He descends on the enemy with a bloodcurdling "Ayo Gorkhali";

And the latter knowing it would be sheer folly;

To stop this drop of quicksilver, and put up a fight;

Downs weapons, and is gone with the speed of light.

He is known as the bravest of the brave, whatever the situation;

He is ever thus - from the conception to the cremation.

MY CAN O' GOLD!

The humble tongue scraper;
And the even humbler toilet paper;
More than gold, are useful to man;
And help him live at ease with his clan.
One is of use at one end of the alimentary tract, dear brother;
And the other, at the other.

A little learning is a dangerous thing;
And gold is badly used when made into a ring;
So drink largely and deeply of Pierian springs;
And melt for a better purpose your chains and rings.

Eating off a plate or paper made of plastic;
Leads to various ills, some of them drastic;
Gold is of value only as dining plate or drinking can;
And so was made into such when metal-craft first began.

For Sir Aurum is one of the Periodic Table's aristocrats,
And doesn't mingle much and sire undesirable brats.

THE PERILS OF GOING TO THE ROMAN 1500

Last week, feeling old, worn-out, and weak;

I went to the hospital, for medical aid to seek;

I was horizontalized the moment I stepped in the door;

And given salt and sugar, by the method Roman Four;

Soon, feeling better, I raised my fingers in a Roman Five, for all to see;

But they misunderstood, and speedily shoved a bedpan under me.

BANKING ON MEDICINE

Whatever its composition, or from whichever land;
The benefits of medicine may be counted on the ring finger of one hand;
But that single benefit cannot be dismissed as unimportant:
Drug dependence keeps the bank account from going dormant.

ELEMENTS OF ENUNCIATION

If you want to utter understandable speech,
Pay heed to what I'm going to teach.

Do not open your mouth too little,
For fear of spraying spittle;

Neither open it so much,
That tips of nose and philtrum touch.

In either case you would be guilty,
Of speech faltering or faulty.

In one case you might be guilty of saying "X-xis";
In the other, of saying "Why yak's sis".

So always strive for the golden mean,
And open your mouth somewhat in-between.

MARRY AND SAY SORRY EVERMORE

• 34 •

He who says "Sorry" when he is in the wrong;
He's called "honest"; to the class of just men, he does belong.

He who says "Sorry" when he is not sure whose fault it is;
He's called "humble"; also, he's polite, and takes pains to please.

And he who says "Sorry" when he is in the right;
He's called "husband"; he's ever loath to ignite a loathsome fight.

LOLLIPOP; OR, LAUGHING OUT LOUD & LONG IS PUERILE OR PERVERTED

After being on a diet for many a dreary day;
I stepped onto my weighing machine to see what it had to say.
My wife stood opposite me, her head over the machine bent;
And soon started emitting sounds of merriment.
"What's the matter?", I asked, with a hefty frown on my face.
She said, "Just look at what this machine says;
"It says L O L, or Laugh Out Loud;
"So stop looking like a field newly ploughed."
I then saw the reading with mine own eyes;
And it was something comforting and nice.
Weight of 70.7 kilograms was the figure;
Which is not bad for a lifelong beer swigger.

SUMPTUOUS REPAST VERSUS PRESUMPTUOUS PASTRY

• 36 •

The work of E. C. Bentley can be matched by just a very few;
He was the creator of the charming, cheeky clerihew.
Though on the meals of Keats and Yeats I have fed;
I've got more joy from the morsels of good old Ed.

SEMANTICS FOR SENIORS:
E C BENTLEY

• 37 •

Edmund C. Bentley,

Wrote rhymes a bit differently;

He picked his victims from history or the news,

Then licked his pencil-point and wrote clerihews.

DON'T BE GLUM, CHUM

Life shouldn't be too glum even in, say, a slum in Ernakulum;
Should one secure a steady supply of some supernaculum.

K.Y.C.

Why do they have the rigmarole known as K.Y.C.?
They are not interested in understanding or serving me;
Out of mulishness and petty despotism they get their thrill;
So tell me, does the K stand for Knock or Kick or Kill?

THE QUACK DUCKS

A quacksalver, in a bid to sell his wares;
Unwittingly adds thus to an irascible man's woes and cares:
"The quicksilver stands at ninety-nine point three;
"Buy four of these bottles and get one free."
But futile is his attempt to make a few bucks;
The man throws a haymaker; the quack ducks.

THE KEYBOARD IS MIGHTIER THAN THE SWORD

Quotidian wifely eccentricities, rebukes, tattle;
Yells, ultracrepidarianisms, idiaminosities, odious prattle;

Abysmal stupidities, deceits, fabrications, gloatings;
Hitlerisms, jealousies, kiddings, lambastings;

Zigzag-moods, xanthippishness & churlishness;
Verily bedevil numerous men & marriages.

Drafted by: Some men who had the F1tery to drink,
At the Space Bar, while exchanging many a merry wink.

Wives, be warned; revenge is being planned by married males;
For you aren't the only sex that exchanges e-tales.

UNWRAPPED AT 20, SCRAPPED AT 50

• 42 •

Said the wife, cattily, "Though I am forty-nine;
"I feel fine, I feel divine;
"You know the man at Number 33;
"He always has a word of praise for me."

Said the husband, chattily, "I know the one you mean;
"His place of business also, I have seen;
"He is a dealer in odds and ends, and every kind of scrap;
"He ever speaks of you whenever he opens his trap."

THEN AND NOW

I oft ponder on Why and Wherefore, When and How;

And now and then, I think of Then and Now;

She was a chic, cheerful chick then;

But now is a hostile, horrendous hen.

What the reason be, I know not, though I have thought enow.

SPEEDING ON A HIGHWAY ON A SUMMER AFTERNOON

• 44 •

The highway is treeless, straight and bright;
And there's not a single gas-station in sight;
There are miles to go before I can take a pee;
Damn, so many miles to go before I can take a pee!
Exults my wife, "No beer, I said. Serves you right."

SNUFF OUT YOUR LAUGHTER, ELSE GAG YOUR MOUTH

• 45 •

Laugh not at your own gags and wheezes;
Remember, it is not the snuff-box that sneezes.

CINDY

An I.T. guy, on his wedding day;
To himself, has this to say:
"Married life's gonna be like a holiday in heaven;
"I'll ever remember my dear wife Cindy, 24/7."

Seven months later, the guy executes a neat trick;
He changes field type from character to numeric.
What was "24/7" now becomes 3.43;
Guy says, "I'll think of her half of a week if I be free."

Twenty-four months later still, fires have begun to abate;
The gorged guy changes field type from numeric to date.
Guy says, "On her birthday, 24/7, I'll think of 'er;
"More than that would be too much of a bother."

A LITTLE CHICK,
A LOT OF CHEEK

• 47 •

Here's a simple single-question quiz -
Step on to the lea and answer me this:

Which famous writer was an authority on chickens?
No, the answer is not Charles John Huffam Dickens.

All right, you've done nothing but sit and gawk;
I'll tell you the answer - it's Stephen Leacock.

TAKE DELIGHT IN DUTY AND DISCIPLINE

• 48 •

Whether we be commoners or kings,
Human life entails two painful things.

What be the twain pains that humans are apt to get?
They be the pain of Self-discipline and the pain of Regret.

However, the former is merely a mild, mellow matter,
When compared to the lethal lashings of the latter.

Remember that tomorrow's lighter welts,
Have their roots in today's tighter belts.

So, self-discipline is a kindness which, to yourself, you owe,
So as to escape future anguish, agony, affliction and woe.

YES, SENSE SAYS THAT TIME IS OF THE ESSENCE

• 49 •

Donate something, be it mighty or just a mite;
Your item may well alleviate a fellow human's plight.

Give in cash or in kind, without waste of time;
Do it before the clocks emit the next hourly-chime.

TONGUESTEN GUN

Never argue with an argute wife;
For she may have brains and tongue sharp as a knife;
Your recklessness you may forever rue;
If perchance she is shrewd and also a shrew.

GOTCHA, BOTCHER!

Should you have occasion to entrust yourself to a surgeon's care,
Remember that the proper way to address him is "Doc-tear".

Should he botch up on account of ineptitude or negligence;
Say "Doct-err, I shall have to ask you for adequate recompense."

DO YOU HAVE DE WITT TO GUESS THIS?

• 52 •

The favourite food of the founder of Reader's Digest,
Was condensed milk - as you, no doubt, rightly guessed.

MISSION TO MARS

You are overweight, it is evident from your massive arse;
A smart way to lose weight is to go on a mission to Mars.

KIN WHO AREN'T AKIN

Of middle-aged brothers twain,
The obese one was a constant pain,
In the neck of his teenaged nephews;
And in speaking to them, used words of abuse.
The other was of the type hail-fellow-well-met,
And was accepted by the boys as part of their set.
How were the uncles nicknamed by the lads,
When out of earshot of their dads?
The abusive one they called "Carbuncle",
And the affable one "Pro-teen uncle".

A HOUSE EVER THICK WITH KITH

• 55 •

The bare floor is disagreeable to my fundament;
For for sitting on sofas the latter is mainly meant;
Since my living room is oft crammed with visitors;
I oft lower my butt to the floor and softly curse.

Their families might start running missing person ads; so,
I wish my drear unbidden guests would get up and go;
Without further ado;
And without even an adieu.

Let them have future powwows at a sizeable aerodrome;
And kindly grant me use of the place that I call my home.

BOTTLE UP THE ONE, UNBOTTLE ANOTHER

• 56 •

He who bottles up birse;
Later, medical expense incurs.

CONSTERNATION AT THE VERBIVORE CLUB

Said a member: "Hello, Joseph; your face is long;
"On your lips there is nary a smile or song;
"And you look like you wrassled with King Kong."

Remarked the second: "Unsteady is your gait;
"If you have a problem, kindly sait."

Spake the third: "Have you lost your orientation,
"Because of an occident?
"Permit me to take you to a medical station,
"And I'll pay the expenses to the last cent."

Quoth the fourth: "You look like Hiroshima after the final raid;
"For your health and well-being we are much afraid."

Suggested the fifth: "Let's play some tic-tac-toe;
"Sit down, Joseph, or rather, zig zag Joe."

Then up spake young Joe: "I care not for nought or cross;
"I just had a joust with the domestic boss."

"Was that all?", the others exclaimed;
"Why didn't you throw a punch on her face, well-aimed?"

"I did", said poor Joe, "unaware that she is an expert in martial arts;

"And she threw me about until, from my ears, out came farts."

ELEMENTARY, WHAT, SON?

Nathan and Clarice met in Rome,
Married, and set up home,
And in due course, with a baby daughter, were blessed;
What did they name her - son, have you guessed?

Yes, I know that quizzes of this kind are bloody bores;
But had you diligently studied your Chemistry and Latin,
You would have lost no time in saying: "Sally, of course,
"Was the name the couple gave their new, little kin."

TAKE PERIODIC INVENTORY OF THE LAVATORY

I called Emergency and yelled that my GHQ was erupting;
Within twenty minutes my front door bell went tong-ting.

Flustered, I thought: "Oh gee, I don't look like the normal me;
"But I suppose I had best emerge and see."

A posse of professionals, mostly firefighters, stood without;
They requested me to tell them what my call was all about.

Well, I told them that GHQ is my shorthand for globular
hindquarters;
They threw red-hot lavaish looks at me, the raging rotters.

They didn't much care to wait and see what would happen next;
They seemed ready and glad to shove off at the slightest pretext.

Later that day I purchased a mini-cartload of diapers;
Though it caused an enormous evacuation of my purse.

I also bought rolls and rolls of toilet paper;
And I hope that there will be no repetition of today's caper.

IF NOT POSH, AT LEAST SOPHISTICATED

Back in the days of the British Raj;
If a Brit got an urge to see the Taj;
He would undertake an ocean voyage;
For tickets, he would perhaps an agent engage.

As he commenced preparations for his trip,
Seasoned voyagers would give him this tip:-
"Know this as the smart mode of travel to and from the Orient
"(The extra outlay is really money well spent):
"Take a Port side cabin on the voyage Out;
"Of this you need have nary a doubt;
"Choose the Starboard side for the voyage Home;
"This tip you'll find in neither treatise nor tome."

Thus, they say, was born a word for elegant and expensive - POSH;
But up North there was a fellow named Alistair MacIntosh;
Who said to himself: "I'll do it the other way around;
"And save myself many a penny, shilling and pound."

Accordingly he sent instructions to his London-based friend Ed;
And shortly thereafter got a telegram reading "SOPH IS TICKETED".

MAIS OUI, THEIR EAGERNESS IS UNDERSTANDABLE

The Thai marriage registrar looked far from sunny;
Quoth he: "The holy state of matrimony,
"Shouldn't deteriorate to aversion or acrimony,
"And end at last in divorce and alimony.
"Are you ready and willing to become man and wife,
"And complement and compliment each other for a serene life?
"Before I register your embarking on a life new;
"Answer my question individually, the two of you."

But the bride and groom full of glee,
Answered, "SIAM" siamultaneously.

SUPPLY GOOD BEERS OR BE SUBJECT TO OUR JEERS

• 63 •

A beer manufactory compromised on quality, of late;

Irate customers went frothwith to expostulate;

Their allegation was at first stoutly rejected;

But the delegation didn't turn away dejected;

They proved to the chief Amoral Larcenous Executive,

That there was more than a grain or truth in their narrative.

The management at last backed down and said, "Do not worry;

"We will remedy matters and restore quality before Fib-brewery."

DRESS WITH FLAIR BUT NOT IN FLARES

• 64 •

Out in the lane stands
the winsome lass Wendy;
She's forgotten something,
she wishes it were less windy;
Her skirt's smart, stylish and mod;
as the French would say, it is dernier cri;
But she came out in a terrific hurry, and of
intimate wear of any sort, her derriere's free.

FAMOBROSIHUWISODA

With just a few abbreviations, as you will presently see;
I can precisely pinpoint all members in a family tree.

Fa and mo are the abbreviations for father and mother;
Si and bro, the abbreviations for sister and brother;
The abbreviations Wi and Hu look like names Chinese;
But they stand for wife and husband, if you please;
Da and so are the abbreviations for daughter and son;
This system can be used in earnest, or just for fun.

Er and et are the abbreviations for elder and eldest;
Yor and yot, the abbreviations for younger and youngest;
Also, there are numbers aplenty;
To make use of them, please feel free.

As an example, my wimoyotsi4da2so, you see,
My wife's mother's youngest sister's
fourth daughter's second son, would be.

The above, in ambiguous language would be:
"Wife's first cousin once removed".
I hope all lovers of clarity can clearly see,
That my assertion is fully proved.

If I say that my yorbro lives in Yarborough;
You'll get it, if with this system you are thorough.

However, use this system only when you write;
Used in speech, people might think that you are tight.

To end on a personal note, I should say I am wiser;
No, not more wise, not a savant,
Not solemn, not Solomonic, not anyone's adviser;
Simply put, it means "Wife's servant".

WHITHER HAS GONE MY JOIE DE VIVRE?

• 67 •

When I was younger my days were full of joy and fun;
And the zest and zing were much more with her away.
Now I am old and I shiver even when I sit out in the sun;
I do nothing much but slowly and silently wither away.

A PAGE FROM THE BOOK OF A SAGE

• 68 •

They asked the old man how he was so happy at his age;
He gave his formula, worthy of his reputation as a sage.

"I assure you, I am always in good spirits," said he,
"I constantly ensure that good spirits are inside me."

THANK GOD IT IS NOT NEXT MONTH

• 69 •

If I say that I am not nervous about addressing this gathering,
I most certainly and brazenly lie;
But I am sure glad that today is not next month,
But just a day in plain, good old July.

AN ILL-USED MALE ESPOUSES THE IDEA OF BECOMING EX-SPOUSES

He has had enough of years and years of being despised and harried;
He's going to have himself de-spoused, he wonders why he so long tarried.

BELLIES BUFFETED BY A BUFFET

Plates smooth and shiny and very havvy;
Such as could be held only by a navvy.

Chairs mighty and weighty, and few and far between;
Marathonic distances to and from the tureen.

A hall that was hot;
A soup that was not.

A substance that was labelled a sweet;
And was more insipid than the welcome greet.

Rice dishes that, on the table, looked pretty;
And in the mouth, were gooey or gritty.

Oleaginous side-dishes agleam in fiery crimson gravy,
That from the gourmet would get no notices ravey.

Gaudily besmeared and ornately decorated desserts,
Reminding gourmands that they were about to get their just deserts.

Ice creams that melted under a stern gaze,
And in their favour had nary a word or phrase.

Conversations that appeared to be desultory,

But really were hitting-below-the-belt-ory.

For the host, a merciless, mammoth bill;
They say that he is recovering from it still.

Such was a luncheon buffet that I attended;
But enough; least said, soonest mended.

A SKINFLINT'S SECRETS OF SUCCESS

Regarding my financial success I'll give you a few hints;
I rose to humongous heights by dint of divers didn'ts.

Didn't feed the hungry, clothe the naked or give to charity;
Said No to all fund-raisers with celerity and clarity.

Didn't try pipe or cigar, or any kind of smoke;
Never bought chocolate, candy, or Coke.

Didn't consume whisky or brandy;
Trained myself not to become frisky or randy.

Didn't play cards or roll the dice;
For lunch, killed and ate the house mice.

Didn't turn on the lights at dusk;
Dined off a glass of water and a rusk.

Didn't flush when I took a leak;
Wiped my ass once a week.

Didn't bathe more than once a year;
No creditor ever came near.

GRINS AND GROANS, MIRTH AND MOANS

• 74 •

Felow-traveller, do you now grin or groan?
The seed you sowed, now has grown.

In fact, everything from your Pa and your Ma,
Is just the working of the inexorable law of karma.

A PRESCRIPTION FOR HAPPINESS, HEALTH, AND LONG LIFE

Every day have something useful and unselfish to do;
Of utilitarian and absorbing hobbies have one or two;
Then, though the body you wear may by no means be termed new,
Your visits to the doctor and pharmacist will assuredly be very few.

ADVICE FROM TUTOR TO TUTEE

• 76 •

Algebra is math that deals with variables, such as a, b and c;
Study well, else your promotion may be put in abeyancy.

AN APOLOGY AFORE ADIEU

I am just a new entrant to the Pen-and-Ink herd;
I apologise for the rot wrought, oft has my ink erred;
And the wrath of purists and puritans I've certainly incurred;
But - my best piece - prim, proper and sans dirt,
Accidentally fell into a pail of yogurt;
And thus dissolved the noblest words I ever penned - in curd.

ENVOI

In assuming the role of envoy from the Land of Fun;

Some I have hurt, some enemies I have won;

But there are others who approve my calling a spade a spade;

And count me in as a friend firmly made;

Do you, dear reader, belong to the latter set?

If so, do tell me; I want all the friends I can get.